BOOK PROPOSAL MAGIC

Essential Guide on Writing a Winning and Selling Book Proposal with a Ghostwriter

Written by Jeffrey A. Mangus

Copyright

Ghostwriting USA/JAM Books 2020© All rights reserved. No part of this publication may be reproduced, stored in a retrieval system, or transmitted in any form or by any means—for example, electronic, photocopy, recording—without the written permission of the publisher and author. The only exceptions are brief quotations in printed reviews.

Published by Jeffrey Allen Mangus/ Ghostwriting USA-JAM Books 2020©
Printed in The United States of America
Editor: Anne Weise

Some names and details may have been changed to protect the privacy of individuals.

ISBN- 9798677679308
ISBN-
Library of Congress Control Number-

Author-Jeffrey A. Mangus CEO-Ghostwriting USA
Http://www.ghostwritingusa.com

Acknowledgments

Thank you to all of my client's past, present, and future. Without you, my ghostwriting life would not be possible.

Thank you to my wife Kelly for always being there, loving me through for better or for worse.

Thank you to all of my kids, Brady, Ryann, Gabby, Jacob, and Sophie. Thanks for believing.

Thank you to Warren Tuttle, Gary Krebs, and all of the incredible authors around the world for helping me get to where I am today with my ghostwriting.

Table of Contents

Copyright 3

Acknowledgments 4

Dedication 8

Preface 9

Chapter 1/What is The Main Purpose of a Book Proposal 16

Chapter 2/ What is the Basic Parts of a Proposal 28

Chapter 3/What is the Ghostwriter's Role in Your Book Proposal 38

Chapter 4/ Collaborate on the "SIZZLE" of the Book Proposal 47

Chapter 5/ Collaboration on the Comps 51

Chapter 6/Compiling Annotated Table of Contents 81

Chapter 7/Collaborating on Book Specs 87

Chapter 8/ Writing the Sample Chapters with your Ghostwriter 93

Chapter 9/ Author bio 98

Chapter 10/ Author Platform 105

Chapter 11/Marketing and Promotion 128

Chapter 12/Target Audience 134

Chapter 13/Book Proposal Deal Killers 138

Chapter 14/Getting the Agent for Your Book 146

Chapter 15/ Proposal to Published 154

About the Author 165

Sources 167

Dedication

I want to dedicate this book to my wife Kelly and all of our five children, Brady, Ryann, Gabby, Jacob, and Sophie. I also want to dedicate this book to my extended family, Thaddeus, Katie, and Allison. This book is also dedicated to my Mom and dad

Preface

When I first began my career as a professional ghostwriter, I was eager and hungry to get started. I found my first client, an agency, and I began taking on an onslaught of work. The agency gave me a calendar full of social media posts, blogs, and web pages. The work was intense, hurried, and I was making next to nothing. Yet, I knew one essential fact that by doing a good job, I was getting paid to write. And being paid to write is a great thing, especially when you are just starting. Competition is stiff out there, and to have the work, I, for one, was profoundly grateful. I knew I wanted to use the experience to hone my craft, with my sights dead ahead on garnering the necessary knowledge to able to write books. So, yes, it is an understatement to say my days as a professional ghostwriter started humbly. First working for agencies, and business individuals, churning out hundreds of blogs, emails, social media posts. I was delivering over twenty blogs and multiple social media posts for the agency, among other different clients and small companies every week. It was rigorous yet, the many hours of writing, working with editors, and office staff provided me with the critical development skills necessary to enter into the ghostwriting book arena. I was stubborn and worked my ass off by meeting every deadline. I took the old adage, *over-deliver, and under-promise.* (I still use this and adhere to this mantra today.) After a while, the social posts became mundane, and the blog content began seemingly to run together as one long humdrum blog. Don't get me wrong, I wrote professional level top quality work for my client. It what I was feeling on the inside that little voice telling me, *"You can do so much more."* And writing books was the answer.

Going after this dream, one day, I approached a good friend of mine, who was a high-profile professional, known globally for his accomplishments in his field about possibly writing a book. To my surprise, he accepted my proposal, and the book-writing journey began. He and I jumped right into it, and within days, to my other surprise, he acquired a literary agent. For him, this was excellent news, yet for me, it placed me quickly into the frying pan as things, this book situation started heating up. The agent was an industry professional, a ghostwriter, and had been an editor had many big publishing houses. I knew that my writing had to be thoroughly professional. He was excited about the book and asked me to write a book proposal. This, my good friend, was the first time I had been asked to write a book proposal, and I was scared out of my mind. Yet, determined, I knew that this was going to be a new adventure worthy of everything I could glean because of the sheer importance of selling my author's book. I did not want to appear like an amateur to the agent, so I studied every book I could find (which are very few) on writing book proposals. Some were informative, and some wordy and others didn't provide the necessary information. I needed to hit a home run with this proposal because my career unknowingly was hinged upon getting this exactly right.

Everything was on the line, hook line, and sinker. I addressed the task head-on and began writing my author's proposal. What helped me was my, and the author had worked previously to write the introduction and first three chapters of his book. This was extremely helpful because, after a few minor tweaks, I am proud to say, the literary agent gave me, my author, and the proposal, the green light. When I finally submitted the proposal over to the agent, I was scared out of my mind. I knew that there was no turning back; it was either going to make it or break my career. For days I was a sweaty ball of tangled nerves waiting on his response, but I was ecstatic—that I had written my first book proposal.

Since the proposal was a go, the plan was for the agent to start pitching the book, and within three days, we had multiple offers from major publishers. After swift and thorough negotiations, my author chose *Harper Collins Leadership,* and the rest is history. The agent noted that the advance given by the publisher was one of the most substantial advances he had seen in a while, and I was over the moon and felt I was on my way. That was my first experience writing a successful book proposal. I have gone on to sell three books with my book proposals both with Big Houses and each one a homerun I am proud to say. My agent supports my book proposals and has told me they are some of the best he's ever seen. However, there are many books on writing book proposals, most touting simple steps to greatness. This is the first book (to my knowledge) written on how to write a selling book proposal with a ghostwriter successfully.

It is in my nature to help others, and because I speak to many different new authors around the country, I receive many questions, and one of the primary questions by new authors is:

Do I need a book proposal?

The answer is a resounding—Yes!

So, I thought what better way to answer this question and help new authors is to write a book revealing the intent and inner workings of a book proposal. My intention is to dive deep, digging up the critical, and throwing away the unnecessary, leaving in the essential, for any author to understand the reasoning and know-how to produce a winning and, most of all, selling book proposal.

Lets' dive in, shall we?

Chapter 1/What is The Main Purpose of a Book Proposal

"A writer - and, I believe, generally all persons - must think that whatever happens to him or her is a resource. All things have been given to us for a purpose, and an artist must feel this more intensely. All that happens to us, including our humiliations, our misfortunes, our embarrassments, all is given to us as raw material, as clay, so that we may shape our art."
― *Jorge Luis Borges, Twenty-Four Conversations with Borges: Interviews by Roberto Alifano 1981-1983*

In honor of getting this book started on the right foot, I felt it necessary to explain not only what a book proposal is, but the main reasoning behind writing one. Let's begin by asking the question:

What exactly is a book proposal?

The answer? A book proposal is a necessary tool to get your book bought, sold, and acquired by any major publisher of your choosing. The proposal contains specific sections, much like a business plan that you, the author, must input to sell your book. A skilled ghostwriter can assist you in writing a successful book proposal, and I consider book proposal writing an essential aspect of my ghostwriting career.

    A book proposal could also be used to garner literary agents and book representation. Before I go further, there is a misnomer among the publishing industry where authors believe they can sell books without a concise book proposal. I am here to put an end to this line of thinking. This is a fact—when attempting to acquire a major publishing deal, a book proposal is— THE only way to accomplish this task. I learned this first-hand when I spoke to an extremely high-profile music artist (name withheld) about his new book. I, my agent, and the author had a conference call and the high-profile music artist, was under the impression that all my agent had to do was make a few phone calls, and he could get a publishing deal. He thought, because of his name and who he was, it would be a simple-as-that task.

He was wrong.

My agent stopped him in the tracks, and said, "*I have been in the publishing industry or over 35 years and gone are the days where you can sell a book with only a phone call. Today, it doesn't matter who you are, a book proposal is a sheer necessity—and damn near mandatory.*"

It is evident that times and things have changed in the publishing industry. What used to be publishing was publishing, and proposals were proposals, each having and standard and integral role. Standards within the publishing arena seemingly never change and become complacent, predictable, and comfortable. Literary agents, editors, and publishers across the nation now understand that publishing a book today is now a different landscape than it was a few years ago. The varying changes include the digital age and the merging parts of the industry-changing how books are published, garnered, produced, and sold. The impact of these changes is apparent across the book publishing industry. There are numerous inconsistencies across the board with misguided and confusing information, sending most new writers fleeing with their heads spinning.

The Self-publishing arena has exploded and has given rise to many new, unqualified, and inexperienced businesses to offer editorial and career advice to writers. The problem with this is these are people who only stepped into the publishing arena just from that have learned from the internet and few books.

However, there is one constant remaining among the significant industry changes. A book proposal is a mandated element, necessary in all regards to secure a book publication deal.

Now, you are here for one reason to learn about book proposals and their intricacies along with how to make it happen using a ghostwriter. Yet, even though I do not know your status, you could be a Fortune 500 entity, Business leader, Corporate CEO, or small business entrepreneur. When it comes to book publishing, the playing field is level, equal, and everyone starts at the same point—writing a book proposal—a task that must be done.

Writing a Book Proposal is Hard—or is it?

Around the country, many publishing entities claim that writing a book proposal is hard as hell, and they are correct in a sense and to a point. Yet, overall, the semantics in putting together a proposal is rather straight forward and uncomplicated. The trick is to do it right and input every ounce of information you can into the proposal to make a robust undeniable case for your book.

These fears that an author cannot write a successful book proposal is prominent, and this is where a ghostwriter comes into the picture. You can write your own book proposal but let me ask you. You can pull your own teeth, yet, would you? No, you hire a professional. If your car breaks down and you don't know how to fix it yourself, what do you do? You hire a professional.

Where are you in your book project scenario? Who are you, and what role do you play in your book plan? Maybe you are a hectic business leader, short on time and energy? Or perhaps you know deep down that you do not have the competency in writing to compose a successful proposal? If this is your situation and you understand you do not have time to write the proposal, or the necessary skills— hiring a ghostwriter to write your proposal is the savvy choice.

Still, as an author, using a ghostwriter doesn't get you off the hook. Even if you are hiring a ghostwriter, you must understand the purpose and components of a winning book proposal. Knowing these fundamental elements of book proposals will keep your current and future projects in line and on task. These are critical factors to understand as a writer, whether you have a good book idea or a great idea. Using the book proposal information affords you to assess the book project from a business standpoint, whether to move forward to putting back onto the shelf. I intend to share my knowledge not only to guide you with the book proposal writing process but how to work and collaborate with a ghostwriter in getting the proposal written.

If you have a great book idea and are solid in your knowledge of the subject, writing a proposal isn't that difficult to accomplish. I believe in book proposals, just like innovation. Much like innovation, an inventor builds a prototype that proves function and finetunes the inventor's knowledge of the product at hand. Writing a book proposal has the same importance as prototypes because by writing one, the material necessary helps in refining your ideas and concepts. The writing of the proposal assists in homing in and finely tuning your message, making the proposal attractive to an agent or publisher.

Remember, the central focus of a book proposal is compiling, in a systematic approach, vital information critical in answering the main questions any agents or acquisition editors will ask plus help you to present your most compelling case for any kind of primary publication. Throughout the book, I will discuss the challenges that many writers face with book proposals in acquiring a traditional publishing deal. There are many different types of articles around on the Internet and in magazines that offer helpful tips on writing book proposals. The sad part is most of them will tell you as a new author that you can do it alone, and anyone can get published just by doing it. This is not true. Even though you might construct a great book proposal, it does not guarantee you the route to a traditional publishing agreement. Please know I am not disparaging your dreams. On the contrary, I want to give you the real facts to help you understand the odds about what you're facing.

Over the years as a professional ghostwriter, garnering experience writing book proposals did not come easy, and expertise in getting a book published wasn't handed to me on a silver platter. If getting published by a major publisher is your dream, realize it will take hard work, dedication, persistence, and a damn good manuscript. Even if your project is worthy and if you have an outstanding book proposal, my advice is to keep it real, keep your expectations on a professional comprehendible level, and rely on yourself to do your best simply. Presenting your book to major publishers, still, nothing is guaranteed. So, throughout this book, my advice is going to be an open, candid assessment involved with publishing and of the book proposal writing process.

The one essential factor you must keep in your mind is that— book publishing is a business. The days are gone where an agent can just give a phone call to an acquisition editor and pitch your book and sell your book just like that. Things have changed in today's publishing world and do not act accordingly. The reasoning is the parent corporations put a tremendous amount of pressure on publishers to make a profit on every book they produce. And even despite this, many books today still lose money and are subsidized by the big bestsellers. So, in the publishing environment, the writer has to think like a business person as well as an artist. World-renowned author, Joanna Penn, has a great book on the subject, *Business for Authors-how to be an Author Entrepreneur.* She writes, *"Authors generally aren't educated in business, focusing purely on the creative side, while tending to rely on others to do that other side of things."* With books, you must use your creativity and also use reasonable business sense. Get in your mind that a book proposal is a business plan for your book. There is no other way around it; a book proposal is a business plan, plain and simple. It's a highly structured document outlaying the specific way your books will stand above the fray. The book proposal packs a wallop as it establishes relevancy, who your target reading audience is, and precisely depicts the reason you are the expert, and the best person to write your book.

A book proposal shows your plan on how you will handle the promotion of your book once it is released for publication. Lastly, the proposal must be written with finesse, and in a manner to convince the publisher, your book will produce profit and revenue. Every editor, at the end of the day, asks the inevitable question, *"Will this book sell?"* To drive your point home, your book proposal must inspire, entice, and exhilarate their senses about the project. Work with your ghostwriter to do everything to make sure your proposal has the desired effect— to get the book sold.

Chapter 2/ What is the Basic Parts of a Proposal

"No book or magazine article is for "everyone," so know your audience, then target them with your writing." ~ W. Terry Whalin, Book Proposals That Sell: 21 Secrets to Speed Your Success

Before we get started talking about the parts of a proposal, let's examine what's what publishers think about initially with a book proposal. Every book proposal has the same elements, and the key is to understand the "magic" your book entails that supersedes other books in your category. When working with your chosen ghostwriter, your job as an author involves collaborating on the Book proposal to the extent that the elemental factors are overflowing with excellent writing and knowledge to "fill out the blanks."

Most publishers see hundreds if not thousands of book proposals each year, yet editors and publishes alike look for the basic essentials that make the book shine. A book proposal, in its purest form, must deliver critical information, including:

- Information on Sales and marketing
- Detailed information on the Book's content
- Sample Chapter of the writing

Your goal as an author is to implement the book proposal with your ghostwriter in such a manner to address and answer five essential questions:

- What are the contents of the book?
- Does the author write well?
- Is the author capable and competent on the subject?
- How will people learn and discover the book?

- Is there an audience, and will people buy it?

Remember, publishers want to be enticed and seduced; they do not want to see cookie-cutter template style proposals. That is the fastest way out the door. As you and your ghostwriter prepare your proposal, start with each section independently and work on only that section until you have it where you want and need it. Build upon the strength of each section until you have a selling proposal compiled and ready for review.

The Basic Essentials

I'm going to discuss every aspect contained within a book proposal, but before I do, I want to point to the fact that by using a ghostwriter, you can save time. A nonfiction book project can be sold with only a book proposal and a sample chapter or two. When it comes to non-fiction, you do not have to write the full manuscript before you attempt to sell it. There isn't anything wrong with writing a full manuscript if this is what you desire to do. Yet, spending months and some even years writing a manuscript that won't sell is a travesty. Izey Victoria Odiase, a Self-Care & Personal Development Advocate, said, *"Work on Purpose – Play on Purpose – Rest on Purpose – Do not let yourself or anyone else waste your time."* Many authors have made this mistake and spent months working on their books only to find that their book cannot be sold. It is disheartening to discover your book idea doesn't have legs. Then rebellious authors push ahead pursuing the self-publishing route (there is nothing wrong with this). Still, they soon discover the monumental push necessary and the extensive work involved in pushing the book out into the world. This can be disastrous for a book to find an audience before the target reader has been defined.

Having your book proposal rise above the crowd takes skill, and this is why I want to highlight the use of a ghostwriter in writing your book proposal. The proposal is a business plan, and the ghostwriter should possess the necessary skills to help you in writing a successful manuscript that provides your editor or agent strong evidence and supporting case to convince the publisher your book is a winning and worthy project.

Most book proposals are divided into distinct sections, which each portion, in theory, should stand on is its own merit. Although each section can stand on its own, the proposal necessitates a compilation to have a strong proposal. Each section, when written well, should be the foundational structure book proposal. Book proposals are highly structured documents, and the essential factors of a book proposal include the following sections:

1. The Title Page
2. Flair or Sizzle of the book
3. The overview
4. Book Specs
5. Author Biography
6. Author Platform
7. Target Audience
8. Competitive Analysis
9. Detailed Outline or Annotated table of contents
10. Marketing and promotion
11. Chapter outline and Sample chapters.

Diving right in, allow me to go over each and explain the role and importance to a successful book proposal.

- **The Title Page**-Easy no explanation necessary here. Make sure the title is formatted correctly and free from typos and clerical errors.

- **Flair or Engaging matter of the book-**In my opinion, the heart and soul of the book proposal. These opening statements must be written with pizzazz, a written in a manner to lure and intrigue a publisher and literary agent

- **The Overview-**The overview is the elusive introduction that defines the significant reasons that separate your book from others in your category and plead the case why your book will sell. Here depict your target audience and show how your book will appeal to that defined audience.
- **Book Specs-** This factor involves creative aspects and the style written and perspective of the book.
- **Author Biography**-discuss in this section your entire biography, pertinent information, and how it correlates to the material and subject of your book.
- **Author Platform**-Author platform is like "Gold in the publishing industry. Define and outlay your entire platform, including all speaking engagements, social media links, conferences pertaining to your field. Dig deep and include your email database, and customer base within your platform. Don't just list the main social sites, do your best to join as many social media sites and groups as you can to include. Publishers need reassurance you can sell books, and the platform is the direct way to establish a book presence.

- Target Audience-This section is merely your target audience or people who will most likely buy your book. If you do not know how to determine this. Talk with your ghostwriter on vetting the marketplace in deciding your ideal reader and
- **Competitive Analysis**-This section also dictates thorough market research. Here, you want to describe any type of books that are competing with you and you and the subject of your book. Here you will locate and search for books that are comparable to your book, and you want to include books that have been published within the past five years, and you also want to define books market position relative to other published titles clearly, and finally, the book is self-published or traditionally published
- **Detailed Outline or Annotated table of contents-** Here, you would create an expanded or annotated table of contents, including intriguing descriptions of each essential portion of the chapter. Start with giving an exciting overview of each chapter. Be brief and keep the writing tight.
- **Marketing and promotion**-This section is vital for your publisher to understand how, when, and

where you plan on promoting your book. Outline the course of action, a definitive plan on how you will help the promotion of your book. Collaborate with your ghostwriter on the plan during the book proposal writing.

- **Chapter outline and Sample Chapters**-This is an essential portion of the proposal. Here is where you need to boast about your skills, expertise in written form. The writing must be captivating, clean, crisp, and grammatical error-free. (Goes without saying). Work with your ghostwriter on creating sample chapters that will spark the interest of the publisher and sell your book.

A good book proposal leverages your odds of acquiring a traditional publisher, but a lousy book proposal can kill a deal for you and kill your book in an instant. Remember, the playing field is level, and you must do everything to rise above the crowd and get noticed. Book proposals are something of a mainstay and a way to sell your book the old-fashioned way by making it an earnest, intriguing and convincing proposition about the worth and value of your book project.

Chapter 3/What is the Ghostwriter's Role in Your Book Proposal

"Everyone is playing roles. Mother, friend, caretaker, friend, boss, etcetera. Every role comes with values and intentions. Identify all the roles you are playing. What are the values and intentions of those roles? Awareness can help you to be more effective in your roles." ~ Akiroq Brost

Many of today's celebrities, politicians, CEOs, Fortune 500 entities, Corporations, business leaders, coaches, doctors, and many other professionals see the need to write a book either on their expertise or know-how in attempts to help others solve problems. Yet, most do not have the time, knowledge, or writing skills to accomplish writing a book proposal and a book. Enter professional ghostwriter. Professionals who have no time nor the writing experience to craft a proposal are savvy by choosing to use ghostwriters. Still, some believe using a ghostwriter is unethical. I assure you—it is not. To keep things on the level, it is ethical because if you tell the publisher upfront, your proposal was ghostwritten along with depicting a strong commitment to using the same ghostwriter. Everything remains kosher. In your proposal, make sure to announce the ghostwriter's involvement. And here is a secret. When it comes to book proposals, from the publisher's perspective, having the proposal and book being written by a professional ghostwriter reduces the risk and betters your odds of selling your book. When it comes to writing a book, a reader doesn't mind the presence of a ghostwriter as long as the author's story, skill, and knowledge are presented earnestly and honestly with full disclosure of a ghostwriter writing the book. The story expressed in the book must be from the person named as the primary author.

Yet, things can head in the wrong direction when you disclose you hired a ghostwriter to pen the book proposal, but you intend to write the book yourself. This raises major red flags to a publisher. Why? It should be obvious. If you have hired a ghostwriter on your proposal and the book proposal is incredible, how does the publisher know you can write at the same skill level for the book? They don't. You have not shown your writing skills, nor have you shown this is possible. In most instances, this will kill the deal. Using a ghostwriter for the proposal but not for the book can appear as dishonest and forthcoming, and a publisher will see right through it. The publisher sees significant risk because in the simple truth after the book is written if the expressiveness and quality of the proposal don't hold up to the quality of writing with the book proposal, your publisher may reject the book altogether. This is terrible news and time wasted on everyone's parts, plus you may have to pay back any advance money if the book is rejected.

Publishers and readers alike expect books to be written by the author, who has declared his name on the cover. Publishers and readers feel deceived when they discover you, as the author did not write the proposal or book. My best advice is never to hide the involvement of a ghostwriter, and the answer is to give proper credit to the ghostwriter.

Crediting the ghostwriter on your book proposal and book is fair and the right thing to do. Remember, publishes and readers don't mind a ghostwriter's involvement—as long as they are informed. This is where a lot of writers go drastically wrong. Many writers do not know how to approach establishing credit to a ghostwriter. Some even fear it because they believe their readership will feel they are a fraud. These notions are simply not correct. Giving a ghostwriter credit is uniform and straightforward by using a simple *and* or a *with*.

For a much better outcome with your book proposal and possible book, clarifying the roles when working with a ghostwriter is essential. This is especially necessary before any writing begins. If you decide to work in partnership with the ghostwriter, then you would use *and.* If you remain the sole author and yet tell your story to a ghostwriter, who physically writes the proposal and book, use *with. With* is used when the author's contributions are disproportionate with the ghostwriter's input. It is a simple decision. Remember to list the names alphabetically if your equal contributors or how you deem necessary. Discuss in detail with your ghostwriter how you, as the author want the book and credit to be established.

Ghostwriter Benefit and Value

The significant role a ghostwriter plays with writing your book proposal is providing the skills necessary to write your eye-catching prose. The sample chapters may or may not be the exact chapters that end up on the book, yet, what you present in your proposal must be written exceptionally well. One benefit of working with a ghostwriting in your sample chapter writing, the experience allows you to evaluate the writer's skill level and quality of writing. Use your best judgment in finding the writer that fits your idea of how you perceive your book and your book proposal. This is essential. A professional ghostwriter should possess critical writing skills to write a successful book proposal. However, not all ghostwriters have written book proposals. Some have not undergone the experience or possess the know-how in writing the proposal.

When interviewing with various ghostwriters, ask questions, and find out their experience upfront about writing book proposals. Find out what they know and willing to do to help you write a successful book proposal. Most professional ghostwriters understand the marketplace and recognize how to research and derive competitive titles. This is a necessary step in putting together a formative and cohesive book proposal that will make editors urgently want to buy your book. Overall, collaboration with a ghostwriter is a monumental first step in understanding the cooperative process and getting to know your ghostwriter. By working together through the writing of the proposal is an experiment to see how the relationship with the potential ghostwriter will turn out. If you need a professional to write your proposal, don't delay or procrastinate on choosing a ghostwriter. Research and find one that fits the style of your book and book proposal and begins writing. Remember, you do not have to write the full book or manuscript for you can sell and. Utilizing a ghostwriter to input your story, skills, and expertise into a proposal will save you time effort and money.

    A book proposal, which involves writing sample chapters, will be the test for writing the rest of your book. It allows you to experience collaboration with the ghostwriter and to give a first-hand account of how the book writing process could be. Writing a book proposal is almost the same as the book writing process—only shorter. You, the author, provides a ghostwriter the pertinent information, skills, know-how on your field of interest that would engage your target audience and potential publisher.

Chapter 4/ Collaborate on the "SIZZLE" of the Book Proposal

"It's very dramatic when two people come together to work something out. It's easy to take a gun and annihilate your opposition, but what is really exciting to me is to see people with differing views come together and finally respect each other." ~ Fred Rogers, The World According to Mister Rogers: Important Things to Remember

Humbling yourself by deciding to work with a ghostwriter on your book proposal is a monumental step in the book writing process. Having a professional step in and write a successful proposal is worthy of mention. Start by working together, utilizing the strengths of your ghostwriter to produce a winning book proposal. Once done, this is the first step in seeing your book being sold to a major publisher.

As you and your ghostwriter start the process, work your way through each section just as you would with each chapter of your book. Let's start with the most crucial section of the book proposal—*The Flair or Sizzle*. Start your book proposal with a knockout punch. You must grab their attention. The first lines of the proposal must zing off the page and hook them. If you've ever been fishing, you would know that there is nothing like the feeling of casting your line, and soon as the line hits the water, you get a hard bite! Flair and sizzle are a standalone factor place at the beginning of your book proposal just after the title page. This is the section that highlights something about your work that is incontestably captivating. You can Telegraph the essence of your work like the chocolate tree tattoo a gift bow or the orange and cinnamon simmering on the stove filling a home with a surprising fragrance or more literally like the curious epigram on iBook's first page. Remember that as you draft other sections of your proposal with your ghostwriter, record your flair and sizzle brainstorms in your folders or documents.

Understanding the crucial publisher mindset influences your writing choices in every subject subsequent section. Follow this chapter for direction, understanding, and inspiration and come back when your ideas have ripened. I will discuss different styles of flair and sizzle that you can put into your book proposal. But just remember only use one or two because you're writing a book proposal, not an infomercial or a full manuscript.

Most nonfiction books start with a narrative that opened their proposals with a few captivating pages of writing from the book. Or possibly the book's prologue or an author's note or an absorbing scene from the heart of the text. This is an excellent way to engage editors when the writing is spectacular, and the author isn't well known. In prose driven flair and sizzle, use blurbs to show that reputable authors admire your writing. Experiment creatively with literary quotations or other seeing setting text and story is what narrative nonfiction editors most want to see first. With promotion driven flair and sizzle established your fame with big-name blurbs, consider the value of sales key points in the form of the bulleted list or provide a short-selling handle or hook. You could also use impressive stats if your platform is your strongest suit.

Chapter 5/ Collaboration on the Comps

"I believe in intuition and inspiration. Imagination is more important than knowledge. For knowledge is limited, whereas imagination embraces the entire world, stimulating progress, giving birth to evolution. It is, strictly speaking, a real factor in scientific research." ~ Albert Einstein

The competitive analysis section of the book proposal is one of the most critical sections in your proposal. It is essential to define precisely what makes your book different or better over existing books in your field. If you have serious intentions to get published, you must know the competition and how well each title is performed in the marketplace. This critical section re what most publishers are the most concerned with and one of the first aspects they look at. Publishers' first point is to determine the strength of the potential audience for your book. Most publishers expect to review five to ten competitive titles. Each of these titles is expected to be evaluated for weaknesses and strengths and define precisely how your is different.

Through my days as a ghostwriter, I speak to many authors about helping them write a book proposal. One of the first things I do is ask them a series of essential questions to understand better where they are in the book process. I ask, "What is your book about?" I also ask, "Who is your target reader?" The majority of the time, unfortunately, I the answers most received are, "My book is a million-dollar masterpiece!" or "There's no other book like mine has been published. "it's a one of a kind." Immediately, this is a red flag. This answer tells me rather quickly that you, as a new author, have not done your homework and not ready for primetime. I do understand, novice writers and everyone has to start somewhere. I get that. However, these answers tell me there is a lot of work going to be necessary to flesh out the author's book and target audience. When working with your ghostwriter, help them define your target reader by doing advanced research on your market. Compile a tentative list of titles to give to your ghostwriter to assist in locating the critical sales numbers of the titles to establish an informative sales criterion.

If you speak to an agent or a publisher, answering in this manner is an accurate indicator, you are not a professional author— or intend to be. Publishers are professionals and must be approached as such, not haphazardly. This is not a good pitch or to get started with a publisher or an agent. In this business, especially when first starting, you get one chance to impress. Much like dating, the first date, even the first kiss will make or break the relationship. You do not need to give the impression that you are not professional, nor have you researched the marketplace. Not doing any research will quickly place the deal at risk. Why? If a publisher believes there is not a book out there like yours, it raises questions such as, *"Why is there not a book out there like yours?" "Perhaps, the market is to small to attract large sales?"* There has to be a good reason because, worse, maybe the topic does not have a legitimate audience for the subject. This, my friend, is not a good beginning.

Collaborate with your ghostwriter to set a plan to execute thorough market research to ideally show there are books with the same target audience as your book that have sold exceptionally well. This is music to a publisher and agent's ears because this indicates a massive potential audience for your book that is eager to buy your book possibly. When you and your ghostwriter, prepare your list of competitive titles, perform extensive research, and define successful books in your category. Make sure those titles have been published with major publishers. Never include self-published titles. (no offense self-published authors)

Review of The Numbers

In today's publishing arena, book acquisition decisions are configured by studying the sales figures publishers are privy to review. Publishers review book sales and numbers by using an integrated Nielsen BookScan point-of-sale system. This is a massive database of every book ever published and their sales figures. Publishers who agree to review your book proposal will review all sales numbers for each competitive title you list. Work with your ghostwriter in compiling the most accurate numbers you can find. Warning…do not inflate or deflate the numbers of any title. Publishers know the actual numbers, and if you do this, the deal, in most instances, will be dead in the water. Publishes and agents respect honesty and transparency. By not reporting the best numbers, could put them in a precarious position later in the process. Avoid this at all costs.

Lastly, through your research, if you discover over four-five titles with If your competitive analysis includes over seven books on any given subject, and all of which had moderately good sales, the odds are drastically reduced, you will be offered a deal. Publishers often see if a market is saturated with existing titles, the challenge is marketing, yet another book being too much effort with that much stiff competition.

Author Expertise and Authority

One of the most critical elements that publishers want to see in a proposal is the author's expertise in the subject. The research involved with a competitive analysis shows the heart of the author and passion for the subject. Publishers rely on the author to be the expert, and this perspective is the sole reason that gives the author's book— intrinsic value. In the publisher's eye, an author must be driven and persistent in vetting the competition. If this is not performed with gusto, publishers know it and, in the end, can and will kill any initial interest.

Coordinate with your ghostwriter in this arena by doing your own research and provide a general outline on the subject. This will help your ghostwriter with the additional research necessary by giving as much pertinent information you can about any different competing titles. The information will assist your ghostwriter in further understanding what makes your book stand out, rising above these other titles.

This is the critical area where you're going to plead your case and show, with finesse, how your book is special and unique over the competition. Research begins with specific titles in your field of interest in the category, and you want to locate the books that have been published within five years. And narrow it down even further by pinpointing the books with the most impact on the industry. Perhaps you're thinking, *why would I want to shine a light and bring attention to those types of books?* Publishers are seeking books that offer new and exciting perspectives compared to other books in the marketplace. Additionally, providing this course of top high-quality research on the marketplace places you in the publisher's mind as a professional author. A thorough competitive analysis convinces the publishers you:

- Adhering to a professional approach
- An undeniable expert in your category and field
- Have evaluated your book accurately, through in-depth self-assessment
- And know well the publishing marketplace and needs of major publishers.
- Proves your reliability and stability as an author.

Proven Audience

The number of competitive titles you locate will prove your book has an existing audience, which shows the publisher—sales. Books in your category that have done well only improve in showing the publisher that your book will stand out and should do as well or better.

Competitive Analysis Inner Workings

Your ghostwriter should know the inner workings of competitive analysis. However, you, as an author, should know the tools to write a successful comp analysis. Competitive analysis should be written with the following:

- Brevity-keep it concise and leave it to only one to four pages
- Must be written in Third person point of view
- Short description of the existing book.
- A concise explanation of how your book addresses the topic better than the mentioned title.

Working with your ghostwriter on writing the Competitive Analysis

Searching for and compiling your list of competitive titles begins with the deep and thorough vetting of the marketplace. Research titles comparable to your specific category of interest. Coordinate duties with your ghostwriter by dividing up the research areas. Or you can assign the entire research portion to your ghostwriter. Yet, this extra work and research will have a fee associated. Speak to your ghostwriter and work out any payment arrangements necessary for the work involved. When I write a book proposal, the fee is discussed upfront. In initial conversations about the proposal, I ask the author if there is additional research included. Another aspect of the proposal I define is if they want me to all the research or if they want to participate. Some authors like to get their hands dirty and be involved in the research part. There isn't anything wrong with that, and it is your choice as the author on which way you want to manage the research of titles.

Assuming the details have been ironed out, start the research as soon as possible with your ghostwriter.

Begin the process by compiling a list of books that are as close to or similar to yours as possible. One key factor is also to search for competitive books that possibly could be purchased instead of yours. Writing a book, just like any other business, and will have competition. In the proposal, you want to identify the potential competition.

Researching for comparative books helps editors grasp the critical facets of your book such as style, voice, genre, genre crossover (Harry Potter series as example- Children to adult) and portrayed through written example.

When dividing the research assignment with your ghostwriter, please make a list of areas you will search for and for them to research. This will save valuable time in getting the necessary information for the proposal. The good news is there are multiple avenues on the internet to find book titles. Market research should not be performed in only one area. Research starts with online searches using category-specific keywords that accompany your field of interest. Besides online searches, you can take the search further by talking to local folks on the front lines, such as local book stores and librarians.

Amazon

Most everyone around the globe knows Amazon as one of the largest sites on the planet for finding most anything your heart desires. Amazon is the first place to begin your research, and Amazon is a self-contained search engine. Start by using a compiled list of different keywords to find various books in your category. Competitive market analysis. Yet, I must inform you that Amazon has multiple changing algorithms. This could prove to be problematic for your search. Competitive titles you discover may be swayed by Amazon's algorithms to show only Amazon published books.

Check and recheck and confirm on this by collaborating on every title with your ghostwriter found on Amazon meet conditions for eligible competitive titles.

There are multiple factors on how publishers review actual sales numbers. When you discover books with sales under 10,000 copies in any format, avoid placing them as competitive titles. Yet, 10,000 copies for a self-published book is a valiant effort. Publishers take notice of books that reach sales of more than 20,000 to 25,000 copies. Publishers key in on the book's sales and upward trends. The big question is, how can you locate these specific numbers?

When it comes to book proposals, mistakes cannot be made. So, publishers take every precaution by stringently analyzing sales figures of books you present in your proposal. Yet, most publishers understand, the numbers you discover may not be as accurate as of the amount they have access too. So, there is some leniency here. Yet, do not present false sales numbers in your proposal. Make sure your numbers are as true and accurate as you can make them. If you do, you run the risk of killing the deal before it starts. When it comes to sales numbers, you are expected to know the market, prominent titles within your market, and knowledge of books selling well. Any book that has sales that have caught the attention of industry insiders needs to be included in your comp section. Use these tools

Amazon Sales Rankings

Amazon sales rankings is a specific local within each book listing page. This portion provides the pertinent necessary to find competitive titles.

The appropriate details you can find under ***Product Details,*** and here you will find the imprint publisher, several pages of the book, the type of book, whether it is an eBook, paperback, or hardcover and what language the book is written in. Along with this necessary information, you will find more essential aspects such as average customer review, which is measured by **Star** rankings. After the review rankings, the sales numbers can be found. These are labeled **Amazon Bestsellers Rank,** which provides a ranking in the books selling history to date. Below this section, you will discover specific categories the books have sold in and their position of rank.

Google

Compared to Amazon, Google is the next best place to look for books in your category. Once again, use your list of specific keywords in a Google search and see what rises to the top. Make notes or save the webpages or screenshots for further reference. Google is a helpful resource in locating definitive books in your category.

Publishers Marketplace

When I first started writing my first book proposal, my agent informed me about *Publishers*

Marketplace. I soon discovered what an integral part of writing a book proposal. This is an excellent complete online database of publishers, agents, and the latest book deal announcements. Their newsletter alone is worth the price of admission alone because they send the announcements daily. The information gleaned from this provides critical information about books being published around the world. However, there is a cost. A one-month subscription costs $25 but well worth it. Each week, you will have insider info delivered straight to your email on forthcoming books that are not yet announced to the general public. It is well worth your time to subscribe to this website and its weekly newsletter *Publishers Weekly.*

Asking Librarians

One research aspect often overlooked is asking local librarians about specific titles. Hit the streets and speak to your local librarians and find out about any referenced titles of similar books in your category. Remember, librarians are excellent sources of information about comparable books.

Actual Reading Competitive titles

One of the most forgotten aspects of vetting the market for competitive titles is reding the books. The next step is to read. Jim Rohn, author of *7 Strategies for Wealth & Happiness: Power Ideas from America's Foremost Business Philosopher,* said, *"Reading is essential for those who seek to rise above the ordinary."* Mr. Rohn's advice is invaluable when it involves a book proposal. Choose the books that are most similar to your books and purchase them, then sit down with a large cup of tea—and read. Don't just skim the pages, dig in, and discover what makes each book work. Take notes on each one and then brainstorm on how you can address the topic with better understanding and clarity. Define how each book is relevant to your book, and record what makes the title less relevant about your subject. Once you have the essential facts of the book, decide if the book has merit and warrants being included in your comp section. Study each book analytically by examining points of differentiation and style, tone, and voice.

Trim and Snip

Narrow down your list of the three to 10 books at best, make your case for the marketability of your concept. Below I provided a checklist to decide what to include in the final list. Remove books for the following reasons.

1. A major publisher has not published them. Small press and academic books, unless they sold well, aren't generally considered competitive period if you find scores with small press books on your subject, write about them as instructed later in this chapter.

2. A traditional publisher has not published them. Self-published books and unless their strong sellers available in bookstores don't belong in your comp section. Remove them. They have not been published in the last five years period although there are exceptions generally publishers want to know about recent books so keep the books under five years in your comp list. They have not sold well. Books on your subject that didn't sell disapprove your market; however, you must address titles published recently by major publishers. Take care to explain factually convincingly and briefly why your book will succeed despite the evidence of similar books failure. This alone could set you apart and strike a deal.

Obtaining and evaluating Sales Figures

Placing too many bestselling books in your proposal can backfire on you. Of course, your competitive analysis should include all books that are leading to sales in your subject area. But you, like most writers, probably wonder what success looks like in book sales anyway, don't you? The answer, unfortunately, isn't straightforward. Sales numbers are considered good yet vary with each publisher as to the format and subject matter along with the context of the book. Here are the basic rules of thumb about publishers. Including actual sales numbers sales of fewer than 10,000 copies in any format, don't generally belong in your competitive title section. Yet these numbers are the usual status quo. Books that have sold more than 25,000 copies over a few years with sales trends that are stable or trending up will prompt any publisher to look more closely. Those books with this sales number are considerable comps. But how can you find the numbers? Well, publishers endlessly analyze specific sales figures industry pros assume you won't have insider numbers. Still, you're expected to know at least generally which books are selling well enough to be on the publisher's radars and therefore belong in your com section. So below, use these tools.

Amazon sales rankings. Research books in your subject area in the format in which you hope to be published. Look for either paperback or hardcover books that consistently rank in the top 2500 or so of all books Amazon sales or rank as must-haves. Books that rank up to 25,000 are worth a second look. In books that consistently rank outside the 50 first 50,000 aren't usually considered complete competitive by publishers. Look also for category rankings between one and 100 double check the format of the book you're investigating rankings may be different for e-books paperbacks and hardcover editions.

Amazon bestseller searches. It may take some perform thorough research to find the top-selling category-specific books period but use the bestselling filter in the relevance box on Amazon's advanced search page in the books Department. The results update hourly in may include momentary anomalous lists big sales but will show you which books consistently appear.

How to Write the Competitive Analysis-Style

The most important part of your competitive analysis is writing it in a formalized structure below you will find an effective structural organization for your comp section.

1. Start with a one to the three-paragraph introduction that explains where your book fits similar relative titles. Show that comparable books have sold well but have not saturated the market in that your book is a much needed a unique addition to the field. If

many related small press books have been published mentioned and dismiss them in a few senses like so many books on my subject, have been published by small presses, but none have been broadly distributed—# 2 list 3 to 10 books in the following format.

2. Book title author publisher publication year format that matches your proposed books format either mass market or trade paperback eBook or hardcover or audiobook current price of formatted listed trim size if illustrated a one or two-sentence description of the book and a one or two-sentence comparison the statement that positions your book showing why your book is different in that a market. Exists for that difference or demonstrating why the success of the book is a good indicator that your book will be successful as well. Remember the comparison statement is a prompt that will help you craft this one,

or two-sentence comparison use these prompts to be able to craft this chosen one prompt the best suits each comparable title remember also do use your own words in your own voice in your proposal work with your ghostwriter on your style and tone it makes sure it isn't exactly the way you want it before presenting your book proposal

Interested editors will verify sales numbers on com titles you list either through their company's records were through expensive software called BookScan. The software scans numbers, while helpful, that are incomplete only showing sales to major retail outlets which amounted between 50% and 70% of total sales you likely don't have access to books can but you should know that it does exist and that any sales figures you provide will be checked so be accurate.

The Mistakes of a Comp Analysis

When it comes to writing a comparative analysis, it is a fan dance between right and wrong. The mistakes can cost you more than you expect. So, work with your ghost rider and provide an essential pathway to avoiding mistakes then your comparative analysis. Don't be afraid to list books that are remarkably similar to yours. This is important and doesn't insult any book on your comps list. Don't be violent, nasty. Chances are the editor who was reading your proposal may have been involved in its publication period instead turned flaws into information book is importing written. Still, alternatively, it didn't explore critical issues that are of keen interest to readers such as dot dot dot. And don't blame the packaging for poor sales of one of your comps the cover jacket was designed by the publisher who may end up being your publisher. Tread carefully here. And don't list too few books. Do not leave out a vital competitive book. Many editors say they feel uneasy when they found out that there are similar books that the author has left out or didn't write about. Being open and transparent is the key here. And don't list too many books period keep it at 10. Do your best to make that number happen.

Yet since I've been talking about all of the mistakes it can be made, let's talk about some of the things that you can do right. You want to provide clear points of differentiation from similar books. And also, you want to list best sellers cautiously explaining specifically why the comparison is appropriate. Do list books in the same format as a book you're proposing. For example, if you found a paperback in your category and you plan on doing a paperback, include it. And do list books from several publishers if they're comps. Some companies prefer comps from their own lists, but that's for your agent to determine.

And most importantly, keep your descriptions short and concise. Be brief and get to the point. Makes a more durable case. But the one essential fact to remember as a new author. That despite everything I have written here, if you're passionate about your project, don't let the existence of a few competitive books discourage you. Remember, nothing is new. That's why you can't copyright an idea. Originality is in the expression of the point of view of the fresh angle. And books breakthrough the noise all the time every single day.

Once again, you're not writing a full manuscript here. You want to find the best titles as many as you can find. You want to establish two different sections within your competitive analysis that are traditionally published or and self-published. Because being self-published is a lot different and will have a lot of different numbers and reviews compared to other books that have been majorly published with a broad with the broader distribution. The first book proposal I wrote I did end up to market analysis, and it took some time. Do you and your ghostwriter prepare to spend a little time in preparing your comp analysis to make sure it's thorough and accurate? This reflects on you as a professional author. An editor number one was the seed of reflection that you put in your competitive market analysis but also show that you have done the work to do diligence. You vetted the market as a professional office. This speaks volumes. Editors and publishers want to deal with professionals, not an amateur. By researching the market, that of the titles educates you and fills you with more knowledge and shows you how ways you can make your book even more unique. This is the area that you need to point strongly to and while the editor or publisher with that exceptional quality that your book will deliver.

Chapter 6/Compiling Annotated Table of Contents

"It is worth remembering that every writer begins with a naively physical notion of what art is. A book for him or her is not an expression or a series of expressions, but literally a volume, a prism with six rectangular sides made of thin sheets of papers which should include a cover, an inside cover, an epigraph in italics, a preface, nine or ten parts with some verses at the beginning, a table of contents, an ex libris with an hourglass and a Latin phrase, a brief list of errata, some blank pages, a colophon and a publication notice: objects that are known to constitute the art of writing." ~ Jorge Luis Borges

I strive to capture the reader's attention right out of the gate in all my books and book proposals. The first page and even closer, the first paragraph should be written to immediately grab the reader by the collar and say,' follow me." This same factor must be employed in the books sample chapter descriptions and annotated table of contents. Most literary agents and publishers expect to review an annotated table of contents in the proposal. This practice is not just for the sake of following rules; an editor of agent needs to see the style and quality of writing for the book. Often, many new authors do not take this section as serious, as necessary— and this is where the crucial mistakes are made. Yet, this is one of the most critical elements of your book proposal. For a publisher, the annotated table of contents is the first view, the first sample, the first glimpse and impression into you, your book, and especially— your writing. Remember the first date; you don't get a second chance at a first impression. The same goes here because if the writing is terrible, there is not a second chance.

Collaborate actively with your ghostwriter and work stringently on capturing the nuance of each chapter description with solid, catchy prose that sets the tone of the book. The tone of the book, the subject, mixed with exciting writing, draws significant interest out of the gate. By executing this well, it increases your odds of a book's acceptance. Don't take this section lightly and deliver dull, lifeless prose. Work with your ghostwriter in making the writing burst off the page to capture the publisher's attention.

Publishers want to see the extended table contents or an annotated table of contents. Some people call this section the chapter outline. No matter what it is referred to by name, it is mandatory and a must in your book proposal. If a publisher buys your book, they do not want to run into massive amounts of doubt and risk with your book. They do not wish to take any chance and want to know precisely what they are buying when it comes to you, the author, and the book. Yet, when trying to sell a book. The publisher has every right to know what they're buying. Talk to your ghostwriter and develop a plan of attack to provide an accurate annotated outline of the book before it is written. Remember, books change during the writing process, Publishers know this and yet, want to be assured the book will start on a solid foundation. The changes are almost always improvements and better during the writing.

Many professional editors will work and guide you during the writing process to help to refine the concept of the book. However, most editors will wait for the completion of the first draft. Once received, the editor will provide comments, suggestions, and editorial notes all in the name of making the book better. A well-written annotated chapter outline delivers a positive perception of the material to a potential editor. One issue most problematic for new authors is questioning how long their chapter description should be? The description can be as long as you deem necessary; however, do not write a mini manuscript. Be concise and get to the point, yet do it with style, flair, and professionally written prose. This is where the ghostwriter enters into the picture by providing the excellent writing necessary to draw the publisher into the book's purpose. Descriptions need to be clear and well descriptive. Many new authors can deliver a vivid detail in one paragraph, and then others do it over a few pages. The rule of thumb to adhere to is, if you feel you need more, you probably do. Be as detailed a possible, yet still, do it with excellent writing. Do not leave anything out.

Writing the outline helps in the organization of your book. Seeing the annotated table of contents written spurs the mind to understand parables that influence changes in your book and titles. An essential aspect when writing your annotated table of contents is that defined clarity is critically important for the book proposal. Describing each chapter in detail with as much thorough knowledge as you can provide mixed with excellent writing will capture the attention of an agent or publisher. Spend time with this section. This is extremely important as it sets the tone for the book and sets the tone for you as the author as being a professional. Work with your ghostwriter to capture the nuance of each chapter. Examine the prose and honestly assess how you feel it reads. This is the time to make sure and not be shy. Assess the prose reads and "sings." There is magic involved in good writing, as I believe words sing off the age when written well.

Chapter 7/Collaborating on Book Specs

"Good friends, good books, and a sleepy conscience: this is the ideal life." ~ **Mark Twain**

Production details are a section reasonably easy to put together with your ghostwriter. Collaborate and determine approximate page counts and word counts, which, at this stage, are figurative approximations. The product details section is where you explain in list form the following:

- Estimated word count
- The date of delivery
- Number of illustrations
- Type of book (paperback, hardcover, eBook)

And at this stage, add any other pertinent details that that need to be brought forward on the production design side.

In book writing and publishing, word count is always an important issue. Wordcount has become a prominent factor because of today's society. Generation "Xers, want things quick— and they want them now. The world, our society, has evolved into a fast-paced rat race where people don't have the patience or take the time to slow down compared to people of different years past. Today, books with lower word counts seem to sell more because of the shorter length of the book. Readers today want the information as quickly as possible. They want to be able to pick up the book and read it in a few hours, while on the beach, or during a cozy night by the fire, or on an airplane trip, rather than taking weeks or months to read a full-length 100,000-word novel. The age of the Internet has brought the reader's attention span down to almost nil. Social media such as Facebook, Twitter, and Instagram, have even soaked up even more attention, leaving most with no time or energy to read a long book.

    I speak to many authors, and one of the main questions I receive is, "How many words should my book be?" I answer, "Your book should be as long as you need it to be." Notice, I stated, "need" not want. In my opinion, a book should evolve over the original writing. The nature of the process in writing the first draft and interviewing sessions with your ghostwriter should be open and free. Do not try to place restrictions or chains on your creativity by worrying about word count and such. Let your book come out organically and naturally. Worrying about word count will only generate a sterile, forced book and readers and publishers will pick up on that quickly. When you write your book, word count and shaping of the word count happens mostly during the revision portion of the process. You must take word count seriously, but right now, writing the proposal, you do not have to worry. Word count is mostly an approximation.

However, publishers do take word count seriously because of cost and the retail price, and most, in the early stages, are thinking about production, packaging, and retail price. When a book has a higher word count or book-length, it drives the necessary costs up, leading to a higher retail price. In today's economy, a higher retail price can slow sales, so the price must be within range to generate a profit. Do be aware of your word count but do not, while writing your book proposal sample chapters let word count drive you. Write your book, and changes and revision will happen later.

The book specs, however, must include a word count. At this stage of the game, estimate what you feel your word count will be. Keep in mind books less than 45,000 to 50,000 words are defined as shorter books, 55,000 and up are considered longer books if you estimate your word count and acquire a book deal. The word count will be specified in the contract. Stick to that word count, but know when you estimate your word count, most publishers understand and are flexible with the word count. If the manuscript comes in close to the predicted word count, you should not have a huge problem. The Book specs page is merely a roadmap of your approximations with word count, so don't stress.

My agent told me a story about a word count nightmare he once had with an author. *"One author I had under contract, was supposed to write a 60,000-word book. Yet, when the book was done, the word count as at 90,000 words. The worst part was the author, sent in the manuscript to the publisher without keeping me in the loop. The publisher went crazy, and almost canceled the contract and demanded the advance back. Fortunately, I saved the deal and instructed the author to cut, revise, and get that word count to a manageable level. I believe the manuscript sill hit at 65,000 words, but the publisher accepted that."*

Collaborate with your ghostwriter on the first draft and revisions of the sample chapters included in the manuscript. Here, don't worry about the word count. Write the book in your style and tone and do it the best way possible. Put your heart into it and utilize your ghostwriter's professional writing skills to generate an incredible Books Specs page.

Chapter 8/ Writing the Sample Chapters with your Ghostwriter

"Either write something worth reading or do something worth writing." ~ Benjamin Franklin

Writing the sample chapters is the "heart and soul" of the book proposal. Here, having a ginormous platform, a considerable business, and significant credibility in your category doesn't mean anything if you do not have superbly written sample chapters representing your book. This, my good friend, is where the rubber hits the road. W. Terry Whalin, the author of *Book proposals that sell: 21 Secrets to Speed Your Success,* wrote, "Hook your editor with a strong opening sentence to bring attention to your writing."

To grab your publisher and editor and accomplish this level of the necessary writing, if you can't do it yourself, requires hard work put in by you and your ghostwriter. Working stringently with your ghostwriter is critical in developing and writing the sample chapters. The words should sing, hit the point with finesse, and make the book extremely attractive to the publisher. Your goal is to grip the publisher instantly, making them want to read more. When a publisher loves the sample chapter, and it grabs their attention, they will, in most instances, want to get behind your book. A substantial sample chapter section makes selling the book to the editorial and marketing departments easier with less risk. Trust me, if you do have the massive platform, a strong marketing plan, and the know-how displayed through your sample chapters, the odds of selling your book are— extensively higher.

Number of Chapters and What to Include

In most book proposals, there are roughly one to three sample chapters included. You may also include an introduction that helps allow the publisher to get a glimpse into your life, your story, and how it relates to the book. The sample chapters once again need to be written without concern over word count or page length. Give the publisher everything you got and knock their socks off. Step up to the plate and swing for the fences. Once again, concern over word count in the early stage is not necessary. Now, hear what I am not saying. I am not telling you to write a novel-length sample chapter with a couple of hundred pages. I am also not telling you to write a few brief paragraphs for chapter. Use common sense and keep each chapter to roughly 7-10 pages at most with good solid word count.

Working with your Ghostwriter

Work with your ghostwriter, writing the sample chapters as you would write the entire book. Write the first draft and then revise, tweak, refine the words and information to capture the publisher's immediate attention. When working with a new ghostwriter, the sample chapter writing is an excellent way to learn how the working relationship will evolve between you and the ghostwriter. Plus, it is a unique and excellent way to review the writing skills of your ghostwriter. Remember, if you choose a ghostwriter and they can't seem to capture your voice or provide the level of writing necessary, move on. This is a business, and the book proposal is an extremely document and must be done well. The proposal could be the ticket to a different life for you, and there is much at stake. You cannot let a writer who doesn't have the skills to hold you back. Use your best judgment, but remember, the first draft of any manuscript is usually "Ugly." My mentor taught me that most first drafts are what he calls. "Franken drafts" I now live by that phrase, and it seems to be befitting to most first drafts. Even this manuscript went through multiple revisions and stages before publication. The first draft of this book (and most of my books) is nasty, snarling dogs with teeth. I work and work to tame the beast into a saleable and clean manuscript, one I can be proud of. And you should too. Be patient with your writer; just keep in your mind the importance of the writing. It is your life, not the ghostwriters on the line. Make sure to work in tandem with your ghostwriter in producing a saleable and intriguing first few chapters.

Chapter 9/ Author bio

"Add bestseller lists, awards and accolades, media appearances and reviews as they come up, and, of course, new books. If you have a website and email list, encourage readers to visit and sign up." ~ Rachel Cone-Gorham

The author bio is an often overlooked yet, a critical element to a book proposal. It's essential for new authors, along with your ghostwriter, to understand the essentials of how to write an author biography. The author's bio is a quick snapshot of who you are, what your business is, your experience, what you are writing about, and, most of all—why readers trust you with the material of the book. , and how you stand out from other writers.

The author's bio is the direct manner in which you show the reader how you are rising above the crowd. Remember, the author's bio is the portal into how publishers get a sense of who you are and how professional you are and what you bring to the table. When it comes to book proposals, it is an integral part of your pitching package and will round out, and support the pitch of your book

With book proposals, there are multiple reasons your author bio is critical to the overall success of your book proposal and book sales. In the professional publishing world, who you are and where you come from matters, especially to your publisher and most of all—your readers. Joel Pitney, A book launch specialist in Oregon, said in a recent article published on Reedsy, *"Reading is an intimate endeavor in which the reader and the author are engaged in a kind of relationship. So, it's important to provide potential readers with the chance to get a sense of who you are and why you have the authority/expertise to write about a particular topic before they pick up your book."*

In your proposal, the author's bio must be constructed in a specific manner showing pertinent details about you. There are must-have elements that need to be included that publishers will be on the lookout for. Factors such as the following:

1. Opening byline
2. The basic premise of your work
3. Outlining of pertinent credentials
4. Personal inflection

Opening Byline

Collaborate with your ghostwriter in writing these sections by drafting your author bio with a brief, yet compelling overview of you and your author profile. Cover every nuance that describes your current situation, including, work, experience, past publications, and skills relevant to the book.

Basic Premise of Your Work

The basic premise is an easy task, although it should not be overlooked or taken lightly. The basic premise of your work is what you are writing a book about, and relevant your experience and know-how is to the book's subject matter. Outlay everything about you, including information about if you have published other books, titles, and publishers if applicable. Explain what kind of writer you are, such as a fiction or non-fiction writer, and go into detail on your experience within these genres. If this is your first book, don't worry, be honest here yet, show your authority over the subject. Give publishers and readers the inside knowledge of what they will discover inside your book.

Outlining of Pertinent Credentials

A critical element to include in the author's bio is the specification of your credentials. Showing credibility is necessary to help publishers and readers to feel justified that you are the professional. You are the one and the reason publishers and readers have chosen your book to help solve their problems, educate, or entertain. Choose only relevant credentials that pertain to the book's subject matter and your experience. Listing your qualifications could be as simple as degrees or awards you have received, or any other best selling works you have been a part of.

When it comes to book proposals, your credentials are essential when it comes to the trust of a publisher and reader. Most readers buy books from known authorities, and even if you are unknown, having the vast experience and authority of the subject drives home your book. This shows the publisher that you are the right person to write the book. Remember only to list appropriate credentials that alone bear relevancy to your book. Leave the other stuff for another book.

Personal Inflection

In your author bio with your book proposal always include personal information. This allows the publisher to get to know you and who you are on a personal level. This helps in capturing the publisher's attention. However, author bios are not meant to launch into a two-hour movie length description of your experience and life history. Publishers don't want or need to read about your first camping trip or first date. When writing this section, work closely with your ghostwriter on the tone here, shining a light on your true personality, yet keep it loose, friendly, and open, showing your personality.

However, shy away from being drab and boring. Write this portion with Pizzazz and let your personality shine through. You want to avoid being bland, cold, and uninteresting. Add information of color such as where you have been, feats you have accomplished, or things you have experienced relating to not only your writing but what makes you the person you are. **Adding personal tidbits of information about you could be the difference and helps a publisher imagine who you are and buy your book.**

About the Author Overview

Overall, this section allows you to present your credentials for writing the book in your ability to promote it. Your proposal needs to be honest, transparent, and businesslike, and an in-depth about the author section is critical. Yet, at the same time, take the opportunity to shed your native modesty and be willing to make a compelling argument that you are the person to write this book.

Chapter 10/ Author Platform

"If your author platform is not well built, you may lose readers to an inferior product that was simply easier to find because its platform was superior to yours." ~ Carole Jelen

Today, the publishing industry has shifted into a new way of thinking. Author's must have an established author platform. Whatever plan you intend to take with your book, whether traditional publishing or self-publishing, an author platform is critical to your book. What exactly is an Author Platform? Author Janet Friedman, in her blog titled, *"Definition of Author Platform,"* gave an accurate description for an author platform: *"An ability to sell books because of who you are or who you can reach."*

When it comes to book proposals, collaborate with your ghostwriter on your author platform as a critical inclusion into your book proposal. The use and importance of a unique author platform started when there was s surge in rejected nonfiction manuscripts by agents and publishers— all because the author lacked an author platform. Publishing, in the 1990s, was just being introduced to the internet, and social media was nonexistent so, then, publishers expected authors to be able and willing to be seen and noticed to sell books. In those years, the most anticipated avenue for author exposure was out in public, either speaking, author signings, book tours, etc. Yet, publishers wanted the author to be able to circulate the word in tandem with the publisher's marketing efforts. Publishers didn't want an author who only wanted to sell a book. Publishers and agents were on the lookout for authors who had built professional networks to assist in selling the book and had a plan to help push it out to the world. This remains true today.

Now, agents and publishers, along with a great book idea, expect an author to have an established platform when a book proposal is placed in front of them. Today, the publishers are also looking for high credentials, expertise in the chosen field, professional networks, and a clear and defined targeted reader audience.

Author Platform Visibility

Publishers expect the author to be visible, and this requires a deep understanding of aspects of your life, such as:

- Where do you speak?
- Where do you appear mostly?
- What regions or areas does your work require your presence?

- Determination of where and how you can reach the people interested in your book?
- How do you plan on spreading the word?
- What committees, organizations are you a part of?
- Where do you attend professionally, such as conferences, tradeshows, events, etc.?

Ask yourself these definitive questions when starting to build your author platform. Brainstorm on the answers and write them down or record them. Once you have the information shared with your ghostwriter to place the information in the proper format within the book proposal.

Is an Author Platform essential?

The importance of having an author platform is, in most cases, what sells the book—or not. The platform is any author social media, speaking events, speeches lined up, community events where you, the author, can connect with potential readers. Along with these mediums, your platform should include, blogs, magazines, media conglomerates you have working relationships with. Remember, the platform must be proven, justified, and should involve everything and everyone in your professional life that can help you sell your book.

Most new authors underestimate the importance of having an author platform. Many self-publish ignoring the platform aspect and stay true to the mindset that the world will come kicking and screaming to buy their book. Without an author platform in place, those notions will sink faster than the Titanic.

Even though the degree of importance of platform does vary with different agents and publishers, all publishers wish to see authors who are busily preparing their target reader audience as part of their career. The obstacle is building a viable reader audience that will help spread the word to sell more books. An author platform sets the stage for things to come as far as readership and building of loyal fans. Your goal is to formulate an author platform, strong that will have a massive impact on your readers. The goal is to have such a profound effect on existing readers; their desire to spread the word is virtually unstoppable.

Author Platform Responsibility

The first step with your author platform is recognizing that you, as an author, now have the responsibility not only to write but take on the marketing role of your book. Yet, to ease the pain, we can look at this from a couple of different ways. Long before the internet and social media extravaganza, many well-known writers, artists, speakers, politicians, and even presidents used their clout and exposure to garner publishing deals. (remember, many used ghostwriters). Today, the problem is with the differing amounts of distorted information out there, instructing many new authors to place social media and marketing ahead of the actual book writing. The mindset to use a half-written book to lure and form a generic database platform— should be forgotten. This is a perfect example of the adage, *"The cart before the horse."* It will not work

Author platforms are not bought and not formed overnight. They must occur naturally. Your author platform will take shape form hard work, and drive experience, and level of expertise. Organically, if you have dedicated your life to your career and skill, naturally, you will have built relationships with a variety of people who are influential in your area of interest. These are the key to exploding your author platform and building a solid foundation in which to use for your book. If you are just getting started, keep going, use what you have in your book proposal, yet, do not inflate the numbers. Be open and transparent and instruct on the proposal of your plan on building your platform.

Working with your ghostwriter, only use the elements of your platform that are the most intriguing and impressive. If possible, leave out those elements that are lacking. So, what features are needed to build a platform, and what tasks must be done to start building?

Building an author platform building requires consistent, persistent effort to have a robust viable platform. If you haven't started, today is the day you need to begin. Every day, once you start, work in achieving small increases in broadening your network. Building a platform is about doing what is necessary to garner significant attention to what you are doing and not about requesting attention or support from others.

To get started, there is a multitude of ways to grow your platform. Make sure to include these factors in your book proposal and do your best to be transparent about each section. Start by writing and publishing your own works either in outlets such as magazines, local newspapers, where your target readers will recognize you. If you are in the position where you are not skilled at writing or don't have the time, utilize your ghostwriter to start your platform campaign by writing these in your business.

Have your ghostwriter help you by writing a series of works all pertaining and targeting your intended audience. I call these "Breadcrumbs." Remember when you were a boy scout or girl scout, and they taught you not to get lost, leave a trail of breadcrumbs? These works have the same impact and affect. Create a series of blogs or e-mails and even newsletters and social media posts. Keep your message precise and clear, and post these works over your social network. Stay on schedule and keep leaving the breadcrumbs for people to follow you, and each day, your platform will grow. I started a weekly blog, and it has helped my business tremendously. Each week, I get to relax and talk shop, all about ghostwriting and working with a ghostwriter. (http://www.anchor.com/ghostwritingusa

Take some time and learn how to podcast. Podcasting has grown exponentially and is now one of the fastest-growing mediums to get your name out there. Plus, podcasting is an excellent "breadcrumb" as now Google and other search engines are now spidering for content and including podcast titles and transcriptions. Create a schedule for a podcast along with pertinent topics and adhere to the program's schedule. Consistency is the name of the game here.

Do you remember where you were when MTV came on the airwaves?

I do.

I remember like it was yesterday. I had visited a friend, and we walked into his brother's room. His brother was glued to the television. "What are you watching?" I asked. "MTV!" he shouted. "Man, this is the best station ever!" This was Saturday, August 1. 1981, and the channel started with the phrase, "Ladies and gentlemen, rock and roll!" Oddly and strategically, the first music video played on MTV was "Video Killed the Radio Star" by The Bugles. Remember the song Video killed the radio star?

That wasn't a lie. It did. Video emerged, and everything changed— and it hasn't relented yet. Video for your business is now an essential aspect of leaving "breadcrumbs" across the internet in building a platform. Record Videos and place yourself on a consistent publishing schedule with topics for your videos. I suggest coordinating each podcast, blog, and video with the same topic so you can hit many areas with one shot. Weekly, I organize my topics and shows. The focus allows me to dive deep into the subject matter and provide in-depth information to my target readers and listeners. Building a platform isn't easy, and it takes dedication and intense work, but once you start, you will find the work enjoyable and rewarding as you find new readers and customers, which in the end always helps sell books. Yet, understand nothing like this happens overnight, and to build a gathering of quality audience or in the least, people who are interested in what you have to say is a process of long term.

Platform building is not a cookie-cutter process and is a natural progressing process dependent upon the work put into the endeavor. Every author will have a different platform, yet, in your book proposal, there are specific sections that must be included. Remember, there is no formal checklist. However, below, I am going to list the essential parts of a book proposal.

List out each section of your platform in which you have fully emerged and those that include respectable numbers. Under each heading of the section, collaborate with your ghostwriter on writing what you have done and accomplished under each that would entice buyers to read and buy our book. Use the following sections:

- Pertinent Professional Credentials
- Online and traditional media (Blogs, TV, Radio, newspapers)
- Literary media (Current and past books if applicable)
- Social media- (email databases, subscriptions, website/s, Instagram, Facebook, Twitter, Pinterest, LinkedIn)
- Speaking Events
- Awards and Certifications
- Business and Personal Network (access to organizations etc.)

Pertinent Professional Credentials

My agent says that professional or academic credentials are absolutely mandatory in a book proposal. These are essential aspects if you are seeking representation with an agent or publisher. Over the years of writing multiple books, my path crossed a prolific author with significant professional credentials. The author was globally known and had multi-million-dollar successes in his business. Yet, as I wrote his book proposal, it became apparent we needed to outline the exact portions of his extensive list of credentials. His agent instructed me, as the ghostwriter, to make sure to include every relevant credential in the proposal. "These are the must-haves in the proposal," he said. Now, after selling multiple books with my book proposals, I know an author's professional creds are essential and virtually, the glue to a successful proposal.

Chuck Sambuchino, author of Create Your Writer Platform: The Key to Building an Audience, Selling More Books, and Finding Success, said, *"Book authors are born where credentials meet platform."*

An author's credentials are at the top of the list to include in a book proposal. Publishers want to see quickly how wide the reach an author has in potential book sales. Selling your book to a traditional publisher large or small, an author must demonstrate strong credibility in their field. Publishers expect writers to have a full grasp with in-depth knowledge of what they're writing about. This is essential to establish with any reading audience and must be solidified when it comes to book sales. Readers will not buy a book from someone who isn't prolific in their skills and possess professional credentials. The book will not be authentic if written by a novice in the field or category. Readers want to know the author has the answer, and the main thing to remember here, is even if you haven't finished college or what you have learned is straight from the school of hard knocks, do your best to demonstrate you are the right author for the book. Show you have the skills through real-world experience and be open and honest about how you acquired your skillset. Publishers will respect honesty, and the risk is lessened with higher and stronger credibility. It goes a long way.

Only choose the essential aspects to your credentials that will have the most effect on any potential publisher, agent, or reader. Here, the old saying, "Include everything but the kitchen sink" doesn't go over well. This philosophy doesn't work in a book proposal. Choose what to include by assessing whether the credential aggressively helps you reach readers. Remember, coordinate with your ghostwriter by providing a list of credentials such as leadership roles, professional organization memberships, or any trade organizations related directly to your field.

Media outlets- an author's platform should consist of newspapers, podcasts, periodicals, blogs, and any radio show you participate frequently. This is the section of the proposal that should include only those traditional and online media outlets that you regularly write for or appear. The goal is to accentuate the size audience that you are exposed to regularly. Remember to make sure to add media outlets where you are the primary resource on your subject or skill set. It doesn't matter if you are not a celebrity or are known widely in public. Include everything, large or small, because everything you are involved in matters when it comes to book sales.

Work with your ghostwriter defining this information by drafting a few introductory sentences introducing any pertinent details on the frequency of your appearances, the outlined list of types of media outlets, and any insight into the platforms associated with each outlet.

Past and Current Books

Whether you write fiction or nonfiction, depicting any current books or titles, articles you have published under your name is an essential aspect to include. Show any book you have written to present to the editor your work and show that you have some experience in the book publishing arena. Make sure to outline any sales and the targeted audience. Don't be shy, even if your audience was smaller, any numbers here can be vitally important.

Social Media Outlets

Social media is a hot topic and seems to be getting hotter. For the last fifteen years and social media has grown leaps and bounds, and having a sizeable identifiable platform is critical. Having a strong social media presence can be the difference in making the deal or not. Again, publishers want to alleviate risk and defining your present social media activity, helps in understanding the potential audience for your book.

The more reliable, the better, the more connections and colleagues you can present, the better. Remember, not only sites like Facebook, LinkedIn, and Twitter should be included; list your immediate email databases, website/s, and other access to other viable platforms. Everything counts and leave nothing out.

Speaking Events

Many business leaders include speaking as a part of their business model. Any speaking event is an opportunity to sell books and spread your name. This is good business with most publishers, and when an author has speaking as part of their arsenal, the odds of selling the book drastically increases. Include any scheduled speaking events and list the organization's official name and destination and date of each event. It cannot hurt to approximate the attendance yet be truthful and don't exaggerate.

Awards and Certifications

A book proposal is a time and place to "Toot your own horn" and describe in detail any awards or certificates you received in your field. Remember to include the entire list and, if possible, show the importance and influence others have received with each award honored.

Business and Personal Network

Major publishers want to see you have the power to spread the word about your book. They will want to get the word out early and start gaining momentum. Books, just like anything else, whether its music, a new record or movie, all get their fame from old fashioned "word of mouth. We have all heard, "Have you seen that series on Netflix? It's awesome?" or "Have you read that book by "X"? "Don't…it was a pure letdown." Word of mouth is excellent marketing. Still, word travels fast and bad word of mouth travels even faster. Yet, your personal and business network will be integral to your book's success and the selling of your book. When it comes to your book and spreading the word, your business and personal networks are essential to any potential publisher. They will utilize the chain of people who can help promote the book. Remember to provide access to any of your networks and show the numbers of people affiliated with each organization.

The author's platform is essential, and brainstorming on every aspect listed here will assist in selling the book. Work with your ghostwriter defining each portion of your platform. Remember, your platform is an initial innovative exercise and should compare to the actual book you write. The platform must be concise within your proposal, and you'll need to use your ingenuity and imagination, along with diligence, in building a robust platform. You, as a new author, should be aware of the intrinsic value of the platform. When your platform is professionally managed, updated, and built from the ground up, to a publisher, it is the heart of the book proposal. By displaying a thorough and well-thought-out platform section, this demonstrates massive dedication, drive, and tenacity toward the success of your book, and most of all— toward your author career.

Chapter 11/Marketing and Promotion

"...the work of promoting the book requires just as much work as writing the book, if not more so." – Adam S. McHugh

Marketing and promotion must be outlined as a roadmap of your intentions and plans to market your book. An excellent author friend, John S., said, when he was writing his first book proposal, "I'm not a marketer…I'm a writer damnit!" Even though he was perplexed, I told him, "To sell your book, my friend…you must become a marketer." This rule applies to you. If you are new to the business, understand that promotion and marketing of your book are critical to success. You may ask yourself, "Hey, isn't that what the publisher is for?" The answer is a resounding…Yes…and no. Publishers get deep into the marketing of their books, yet, in today's publishing world, they expect an author to get involved equally.

Publishers get excited when a book proposal is filled to the brim with factors that show how the author will market and promote the book. Your show of enthusiasm in marketing your book can improve your odds tremendously in selling your book. Yet, many authors are perplexed at the sheer notion of doing heavy lifting alongside the publisher. Many want just to write and let things fall where they may come with sales and promotions. This is the wrong thinking and a disastrous approach. I mean, to a degree, I get it. Writers are writers, and most (like me) have an incessant need to write to feel normal. Marketing and promoting are like running their typing fingernails over a dirty chalkboard. Just the thought sends chills down their spines. Many new authors, if not in business already, approach the task kicking and screaming—and I can see why. Because authors are writers, and most are not salesmen. If not in business, many authors are not good at self-promoting themselves. Quite the opposite, writers are introverted mostly because writing is a solitary occupation. The thrill is seeing black on white, words of greatness appearing on their little machine. This is the excitement and the glory, and it is lightyears away from being a publicist or press agent. Author and marketing strategist, Paula Krapf, once wrote, *"Most of us wouldn't cook an entree for the first time without following a recipe and having a marketing plan for your book can make the difference between success and falling flat."*

    So, to ease the learning curve, and alleviate the dilemma, you must put don another thinking cap and develop a strategic marketing plan for your book after publication. Whether or not you like it, the fact remains, you will have to assume other roles, other than writing to market your book to success. I can see your author's mind churning. I bet you are asking, why don't you just self-publish? If I have to do the marketing, why don't I just self-publish take home more money? In being open, I don't have the right answer for you here. Traditional and self-publishing are both viable options, and yes, you can go the Do-it-Yourself route, as long as you know that either way, there is marketing and promotion involved even more so with self-publishing. Major publishers have distribution channels and experience in pushing books to the masses with proven techniques and relationships with the industry. Self-publishing is what I did with this book and other books that I publish. Yet, ask me how challenging it is to promote, market, and strategize all by myself and still have time to write? It is painful beyond words. I have come to terms with the constant need to market my books. For me, this is just part of the business, and you, as a new author, should get on board quickly with this mindset. The train will leave the station and leave you on the platform.

After writing for major publishers myself and for many authors around the country, I've learned a lot about how major publishers think with books and promotions. Most major publishers have found that most of the marketing and promotion take place 4 to 6 months before the launch day. Keep this in mind when drafting this portion of your book proposal. Book authors are expected to contribute sizeable amounts of time and effort toward the promotion, so include the essential "will dos." These are the exact things you are dedicating to performing and will adhere to help sell the book. Publishers want to be assured you will execute according to your plan. Be specific on how you will budget your promotion for the book. Give detail on the amount such as, "I will spend three thousand dollars on these specific tasks." Be accurate on how you will spend your own money. Publishers love seeing you are vested in your book's success. The vital element to the promotion section is to assure the publisher you will make good on all the promises. Be specific outlining what you will do, and most of all—make sure you intend to perform those tasks in the effort of promoting your book.

    A sound marketing plan must be honest and robust, but it also has to be realistic and convincing. Capture a professional tone and speak with authority. Work with your ghostwriter on capturing your voice and style in the proposal. Writing is essential, but an authoritative voice goes a long way in grabbing their attention. Remember, the proposal is all about you and first impressions. It is your job to convince the publisher you understand the importance of marketing the book, and you're committed to doing what it takes. Depict any realistic limits and opportunities that will exist for you.

Chapter 12/Target Audience

"Focus on identifying your target audience, communicating an authentic message that they want and need, and project yourself as an "expert" within your niche." ~ Kim Garst

Among all of the factors included in the book proposal, the target audience or reader is a critical element to a book's success. Additionally, the target reader is vital when proposing a book to a publisher. Having your target reader completely inline will show your diligence, professional vetting of the market, and show you, as a new author, have a defined direction with your book. However, many new authors find this section challenging. Author and Philosopher John Locke wrote, *"In my opinion, understanding who your target audience is, and what they want, and writing to them (and only them!) is the most important component of being successful as an author."* So, understanding your target audience involves knowing your business and skill set and what problems you are solving with your book. Publishers, when viewing a new book proposal, always seek the answer to the age-old question, who is the target reader for the book? Television producer Ricky Van Veen said, *"I think a mistake a lot of people make is to identify a target audience and then work backward into creating a product for them."* Your job is to answer this question and not make a mistake of trying to force build a book around an audience. The subject of your book should be precisely defined to help the publisher understand the target audience immediately. Remember, make sure to include specifics about your target audience, and the key is to emphasize your immediate access and the authority to reach this target audience.

To accomplish this, you will need to perform thorough research of the marketplace and brainstorm on precisely who is your definitive target reader. I spoke about this topic in my other new book *Hiring Your Ghost- The Essential Guide to Find and Hire the Perfect Ghostwriter and Launch Your Book.*[i] A book's target reading audience is not a simple demographic. The target audience as the subclass of people, all in which would have a compelling need or interest in the book's subject matter. The way a publisher sees it is the target audience is those who are willing to open their wallets and buy the book. This is the main reason for performing diligent market analysis of competitive titles. This helps in narrowing in the buying audience of your book. Any potential publisher wants and requires this information in your proposal. Having this information will aid in the publisher deciding on purchasing your book.

Defining your target audience is an essential aspect of your book proposal. Do not put this off to the side or less in this section. The more targeted reader you have, the more definitive audience that your project with your proposal will give your acquisition editor a better understanding and you a better chance of its publishing your book.

Chapter 13/Book Proposal Deal Killers

Talking about the perfect book proposal would not be complete unless I discussed the essential facts on what NOT to do. Working with your ghostwriter, having this information helps you in creating a marketable and selling book proposal. As an author and writer, the information will serve you well in knowing the ins and outs of what to include and what not to include in your book proposal.

One evening, I was driving home from an evening with friends when the police pulled me over. As I saw the blue lights, I looked at my speedometer, and there wasn't any denying I was speeding. As the officer got out and came toward my car, rattled, I quickly jumped out. I began telling him everything. "I'm sorry officer, I know I was doing eighty in a fifty." Please go easy on me..." Suddenly, he shouted.

"Stop!" Don't say another word!"

"But officer, I answered. He stopped me.

"Shut your mouth," he snapped. "I wasn't pulling you over for speeding. You have a taillight out. But since you told me, maybe I should cite you on the speeding too."

I hung my head. I knew I had done it this time I opened my big mouth, and now it is going to cost me.

...I heard the pen stop writing.

"I'm going to let you off and let you go," He said. "But, let me tell one thing for you always to remember. Remember, don't tell too much about yourself." "When you do, it can get you into trouble."

I've never forgotten those words, and in a book proposal, this is especially true. Do your best to say what you need to say, express your point, and stop. Leave it at that and trust upon your words to do the job intended. Long, arduous book proposals are frowned upon, and most, if too long, will end up in the rejected pile. Information repeated over and over sends red flags to the publisher that you have run out of things to say. Avoid long drawn out proposals, unless the material and subject matter calls for the length of information. Even here, write concise and keep it to the point.

Not Defining Target Audience

Late author, Eric Butterworth, once said, *"Missing the mark is one of the ways we learn to hit the target."* In a book proposal, not hitting the mark is amateurish and raises a major red flag, whether you, as a professional author, have vetted the marketplace.

Throughout your entire book proposal, you must depict awareness to the target reading audience in every plausible section throughout. Keep this in mind as you and your ghostwriter collaborate in the writing of the proposal. Your credentials as an expert in your field are only as good as the readers who would perceive your credentials and purchase the book. Showing how your book differentiates makes your book competitive and saleable. Missing the market is a critical error, and you must do everything within your power to make this not happen.

Not Addressing Objection

Publishers review many proposals over the curse of a year. They reject many because the author has not performed their due diligence and attempted o answer the questions a publisher might raise and reject the proposal. Once an author addresses all concerns and shows the book is different, has a unique take that is better than the other competitive titles, this is the way to selling your book. When writing the proposal, understanding what to include that addresses a publisher's objections is critical. What do you anticipate they will ask? Anticipate questions that a publisher would probably ask and address those questions with the proper information in the proposal. An excellent proposal addresses what a publisher might say no too.

Don't Mismatch Author and Subject

A book proposal that doesn't match up with the author's expertise will, in most cases, be rejected. Ensure you do not waste time writing a book proposal that is out of your element. It will get rejected. As an example, you are proposing a book about guitars yet, have never picked up a guitar, this is a definitive mismatch. The only way to make this work is somehow tie in guitars to your experience to make the book proposal work. A marketable proposal will need to have your knowledge and expertise in line with the book you are proposing.

Do not make unrealistic promises

I once made the mistake of telling my son I could buy him a specific shirt he wanted. I promised I would before I knew the price. The shirt was expensive, and at the time, I could not afford to buy it. Yet, not wanting to break a promise, I did everything in my power to get the shirt but failed. I learned never to make promises you do not intend to keep. Avoid at all costs boasting or promising the publisher you will do something that you know isn't realistic or see yourself doing. Stick with what you're sure and confident you can accomplish. Include everything pertinent and doable such as Book signings, book promotions, speaking events, and more.

Adhere to aspects you are either doing currently or know are within your grasp to accomplish. Don't promise things like, "I'll book a whole book tour." Or, "I'll make sure the book becomes a television series." Most people cannot do those things, and publishers know this out of the gate. Include only the factors you know for sure you can make happen.

Don't Be Dishonest

This may sound as if this should not be a factor, but it is a critical element in the proposal. Publishers want honesty and want to feel as if they can trust you to say and do what you proclaim with your book. If there is a section in the proposal you are short on, such as your platform is not large, yet, you say it is. This is a deal killer for sure with a publisher. Avoid elaborating, and don't lie about it. Be honest and say, "My platform is decent, but I intend to work diligently in growing my platform to help the book." Always approach every section with honesty and transparency.

Don't Include Meaningless Material

There are some aspects you must avoid, including at all costs. Do not place in your proposal, testimonials from people who do not have the clout or stature to influence the book. Only include people that can have an impact and affect the proposal, by stature. Testimonials from your next-door neighbor, Bob, will not help. Remember to not input titles in your competitive title section that are not self-published or low selling books that did not fare well in the market. Always refrain from including meaningless articles or websites that are stagnating that no one visits. Stick with only including crucial pertinent information. This is the professional way.

Chapter 14/Getting the Agent for Your Book

"First of all, please, please, don´t go publish until you are one hundred percent sure you are doing a great job, the best that you may deliver. For in this publishing media, it´s easy to get it all wrong when you are just starting. Secondly, find a good editor, or at least a second opinion. You know, four eyes read better than two. You will regret later on for not having a good editor to go through your writing or having a great artist to do the best cover for your book. Because if there is something, I learned during these years in the publishing market, it is to never ever underestimate the power of good editing. And my third piece will be to advise about a good image: the saying "never judge a book by its cover" was created by a lazy author who didn´t give much thought of what really works in the marketing of both fiction and nonfiction."
~ Ana Claudia Antunes, How to Make a Book

We have established that there are multiple reasons to work with a ghostwriter in writing your book proposal. One of the main reasons to acquire a literary agent to help you sell your book. However, this is a catch 22 situation at best. Getting to a traditional publisher takes steps, and the first step is you must sell your book to an agent. The proposal should be crisp and ready. So, how does this work with you and your ghostwriter? Simple, the proposal must be written with intensity to solidify interest from an agent. This is where your ghostwriter comes quickly into the picture. Use your ghostwriter by taking advantage of their skills by working with your ghostwriter to ensure your proposal is sharp and has a clearly defined message on your book. You are the author, and this is the time to not settle for what you feel does not represent your words and idea. Collaborate with your ghost and tweak everything necessary to make your proposal shine and rise above the crowd. This will work in your favor in a multitude of ways. First, if you accomplish this and attract an agent, it is safe to guess that your chances of gaining the attention of major publishers are drastically higher. This all may sound like a massive endeavor, and indeed it is, but not impossible. Many have done it, and many are doing it right now. Yet, keep in mind that most agents and publishers are ethical professionals who make money only when they sell your book. Their skin is in the game.

Jerry Weintraub, CEO of United Artist pictures, once said, *"When you reach my age, you understand that you are a player with skin in the game, no matter what game it is."* A professional ghostwriter has skin in the game alongside you, the author. Your ghostwriter should understand it is their job to supply the necessary writing that agents and publishers are searching for. Remember, the writing must be crisp and on a professional level. I consider it an honor to write a new author's book proposal. Why? Because I see the inherent value and what could potentially happen if written professionally with passion and care. This is what I do. A well-written book proposal can change a person; life, and it alters many lives, including the publisher or any potential agent. It will change your life.

Where to Find Literary Agents

I was lucky in this department. I found my agent n organically through natural progression, and even though my agent relationship happened through the natural order of life, I was not accepted nor represented automatically. It took work and perseverance. I was ghostwriting a book for a prolific author when he garnered the attention of an agent. He signed with the agent, and before long, the agent and I started developing a good working relationship. I massaged that relationship, respected boundaries, and asked a few questions, leaving only essential questions to be answered when the time was right. I knew agents were remarkably busy, and so was my agent. So, I never crossed the line by calling out of the blue or unannounced. Before long, over a few months, I had a book idea and book proposal that I ran by my agent. He loved the ide and asked for the proposal. Within thirty days, the book was sold to a major publisher.

Finding a literary agent isn't as hard as it may appear but grabbing the attention of an agent is a task of significant importance. There is a multitude of online destinations, groups, social media sites, and books that can help you find a literary agent for your book. Remember, do not approach this step haphazardly. This is a crucial step, actually getting an agent. Why? Locating the right agent that fits your book and your personality is critical to the book's success. Employ your ghostwriter to use their existing research skills to find any potential literary agents. Most ghostwriters possess investigative skills and note-taking organization.

Some of the first places to find an agent include:

- Literary Agents of North America
- Writer's Marketplace
- Publisher's Weekly
- Literary Market Place

There are various organizations to search, including directories, and keep an open mind as you may get referrals from colleagues and friends to a suitable agent.

Once you and your ghostwriter begin the research, generate a master list of potential agents, along with any agent, you may have a connection from pre-existing relationships. Take your list and examine the variables on which agent you should reach out to. The next step is to work with your ghostwriter on drafting a suitable query letter to send to your list of agents. Once again, make sure the query letter is written concise and professional. There is no room for error at this stage of the game.

It is exciting to start the search for an agent for your

book. Yet, remember, if you drum up interest and an agent is agreeable to see the proposal, it is only the beginning. Interest does not constitute acceptance that they will represent you or your book. But generating interest is an excellent start. Be humble and keep pushing forward. When an agent expresses interest and wants to sign you and represent you, it is time to start putting it all together. Remember, agents work on books on a project-by-project basis, and if you sign, it will be your decision whether you offer the next book to the agency to represent. Most authors give the courtesy, especially if the agent did well for them, yet, if the agent does not show much interest in selling your book, after signing, think twice about signing with them again. If this happens, shop around again and repeat the process.

Finding a publisher is a tedious and monumental task. Still, the primary question, which seems to point back to the ever-present elephant in the room, do you need a literary agent? Frank Sinatra once said, *"Hell hath no fury like a hustler with a literary agent."* This reality may be harsh but understand, as an author, to pursue traditional publishing, whether fiction or non-fiction, it is mandatory to acquire the attention of a literary agent. An agent is necessary to pitch your book proposal to handpicked editors in midsize to Big Five publishers. Getting a deal with a major publisher, gets you, the author, in the door of bigger houses and helps in the future with other books. Fiction writers who choose to follow the traditional publishing must have a literary agent. Non-fiction authors, especially those writing memoirs, histories, and biographies, need a literary agent for representation.

Chapter 15/ Proposal to Published

"I still encourage anyone who feels at all compelled to write to do so. I just try to warn people who hope to get published that publication is not all; it is cracked up to be. But writing is. Writing has so much to give, so much to teach, so many surprises. That thing you had to force yourself to do---the actual act of writing---turns out to be the best part. It's like discovering that while you thought you needed the tea ceremony for the caffeine, what you really needed was the tea ceremony. The act of writing turns out to be its own reward." ~ Anne Lamott

Every book proposal and agent acquisition are the first part of the book process. The next essential step includes clarifying your plan of which publishing route you intend to take. Finding a home for your book is the primary purpose of writing, and the book proposal is the vessel in which will carry your words and ideas elsewhere. Yet, to make the book proposal generate the sizzle it is intended, you must plan accordingly which route you intend to pursue with your book. This "book map" or plan is the same as planning your business. If you were to start a new business, you would create a business plan to follow to make sure your business stays on track. This is the same as your book. In planning your book, drafting a proposal keeps you on track, and it allows you to follow the process to help your book be successful.

George Bernard Shaw wrote, *"I finished my first book seventy-six years ago. I offered it to every publisher on the English-speaking earth I had ever heard of. Their refusals were unanimous: and it did not get into print until, fifty years later, publishers would publish anything that had my name on it."*

Pursuing any major publisher such as Harper Collins, Simon & Schuster, will be a significant undertaking and, once again, essential to know that an agent must be involved. You will have an impossible time gaining access to editors of these publishing houses without an agent, so save your time and effort and do not try. Remember, smaller or mid-sized publishing houses may accept unsolicited or unrepresented manuscripts. The key is to vet the market place first for agents and the next publishing houses you intend to pursue. Follow the publisher's guidelines to the letter. Sara Paretsky, an American author of detective fiction, said, *"The best source for finding an agent is called Literary Agents of North America. It's a complete list of agents, not only by name and address, but by type of book they represent and by what their submission criteria are."*

I was amazed at all the work my agent did for me right out of the gate. Before he became my agent, I was ghostwriting a book for a new author. The author, being high-profile, sought representation and found an agent. The agent didn't know me yet; he still insisted on writing a book proposal so he could pitch it to different publishers. I began, and I did very well with my first book proposal as the agent provided helpful tips and guidance, and with his help, my very first book proposal sold to one the Big-five publishers' Harper Collins. To say I was proud would be an understatement. Yet through the process, I learned that the agent wore many hats and provided delicate and precise guidance into the book publishing world.

Since literary agents are essential to your book's success, it is only befitting that you should understand what an agent does to earn their commission. Knowledge of the varying roles many literary agents assume will help you in the book acquisition process. Agents take on a multitude of varying roles when an author is signed for representation. Roles such as:

Commission- Most agents work off of risk and take you on as a client for a 15% commission. Most agents work and do not get paid until the book is published. Often, this may take a long duration, and this is why, as an agent, there is an apparent risk in an author and bookselling.

Middleman-An agent's role is to be an intermediary between you, the author, and the publisher along with the vast book reading marketplace.

Marketing Assistance- Agents around the world want your book to succeed. Their livelihood depends on it so that most agents will help in the marketing of a book for an author. An agent will deliver marketing advice and help you with personal and book branding. The direction will be given on increasing your platform, along with bridging the gap between your platform and other influential people's platforms.

Overseeing Financial Issues- My agent is skilled and savvy when it comes to protecting delicate financial issues. His approach is straight forward and never beats around the bush. Good agents ensure your rights are protected to all of your literary works. If your book lends itself to cross-sell into movies, there are licensing rights for audio, eBooks, and even different regions of the world with translations. You will thank your agent for protecting you in all of these matters and your financial security.

Acquisition Manager- A literary agent's primary role is negotiation, and during the negotiation, there is a strategic play on submitting your proposal to different publishers. This encourages excitement and could result in bidding wars for your book manuscript. This is a good thing, and your agent will know how to handle these situations on your behalf. Negotiating with publishers is a fine art and getting a publisher to say yes is a highly sought-after skill.

Negotiation of a Book Contract- Once you receive yes from a publisher, this is where your agent truly earns their money. A good savvy agent will negotiate the deal to arrive at the best possible contract for all parties. A contract must be agreed upon by everyone, and a good agent will work the talks, making sure you are protected and given the best possible deal for your book.

Representation- Agents are there to help you with any questions or concerns with your editor and publisher. They will answer every question on financial matters, and if there are any discrepancies, the agent will take care of the matters on your behalf. When it comes to financial issues, an agent will oversee all royalties, payments, and advances. My agent handles all royalties and advances. He is also responsible for getting checks issued and keeping track of all the paperwork.

Smaller and Mid-size publishers are the houses, that are large enough to matter but still not as prominent as the Big Five publishers. Even smaller and mid-size houses have reached a point where they will not accept unrepresented work by an agent. I have learned through my ghostwriting experience that smaller publishers have the same process as the Big Five, where editors and acquisition editors are looking for book proposal manuscripts represented by an agent.

Query Letters

As we discussed briefly earlier, approaching an agent is the same as reaching a major publisher. Writing a query letter with your ghostwriter is an aspect essential of acquiring an agent. The letter must be written professionally, adequately formatted to gain the interest of an agent. The best way to capture the attention of a literary agent is first, to have your book concept nailed down. Be honest and assess the content of your book, whether it is highly commercial or has a sustainable and proven market.

Always send a query letter to an agent and be polite and professional. Make sure the query is one page and describes your book idea thoroughly, descriptively, with finesse. Keep it concise and to the point but write with flair. Do everything within the letter to raise attention but do it professionally with style. After you send in the query, be patient. Do not be pushy or unprofessional. This is the quickest way to receive an affirming "no." And while I'm talking about getting a no. Always remain professional and accept any "No" and move on. Displaying anger or being overly assertive after the "no" could shed a negative light on you as an author. Remember, the literary world is exceedingly small, and agents and editors do talk. You do not want to get a bad reputation as it will have adverse effects and squash a budding career. Prove you will be a good author, be professional, amenable, and be open to suggestions and constructive criticism. Make plans to have your author platform up and running if you plan when contacting new potential agents. Use every source within your platform as leverage to capture the attention of an agent because an author platform is instrumental in acquiring representation and a major publishing deal. If your platform is smaller but growing, be honest and say that, be open, and let them know your intention to keep working on building your platform and social media presence.

Through your endeavors, you will be met with obstacles, challenges, and rejections, yet remember this essential fact; Always keep going in pursuit of your book dream— and never give up. By following these simple rules of engagement, you should generate a saleable book proposal that you can be proud of. Use it to garner interest and gain ample opportunities with many successful literary agents' publishers. And, I'll say it one more— never give up, stay on track, and meet every rejection with optimism and hope. Study your approach and tweak whatever needs to be fixed, as one day you will thank yourself in following your pursuit, and never throwing in the towel. Words transport the reader into your world, with time and place. Open up and let the reader in, give them a taste, a small peek, into your world with your words. The world deserves your book, and you deserve to write it so— keep following your dreams.

About the Author

Jeffrey Mangus has ghostwritten business books for many independent business authors and some BIG-FIVE Publishers, including HARPER COLLINS, HARPER COLLINS LEADERSHIP, ROWMAN & LITTLEFIELD, and HIGHBRIDGE AUDIO. He is the author of his new upcoming book AMPOSSIBLE (2021) for Rowman & Littlefield and represented by Literary Agent/ Gary M. Krebs of GMK Writing and Literary Services.

Jeffrey brings over 25 years of experience as a business writer, ghostwriter, and blogger, with many published books and eBooks. Jeffrey delivers to every new author real-world experience, expertise, dedication, and extreme professionalism to every word on every page on every book assignment.

Jeffrey specializes in ghostwriting for business leaders, business owners, entrepreneurs, celebrities, musicians, politicians, CEOs, literary agents, major publishers, and corporate entities with ideas and dreams of having a book or multiple books dedicated to their specialties and skills.

On a personal note, Jeffrey was a professional touring musician. He has recorded four albums and was signed to two independent record labels. Jeffrey and his band STEEL ROSE headlined the sunset strip (1988-1992) playing historical venues such as the Whisky-a-Go-Go™, The Roxy Theatre™, and world-famous Gazzari's™. He toured the country and opened for significant rock groups and headlining acts such as Molly Hatchett®, Black Oak Arkansas®, Little Feat®, Jackyll®. And Jeffrey opened for many famous blues artists, Bryan Lee, Jason Ricci, and The New Blood and Chicago Blues Artist of the Year Nick Moss.

Jeffrey worked in the healthcare field in cardiovascular surgery as a perfusion technician for twelve years. He is a retired broker/owner of two multi-million-dollar real estate companies and enjoyed a 14-year real estate career before turning to a full-time ghostwriting career.

If you would like to learn more about Jeffrey A. Mangus and his ghostwriting services, Schedule a FREE no-obligation book consultation. Please visit http://www.ghostwritingusa.com or contact him by writing ghostwriterusa1@gmail.com

Sources

i
https://www.amazon.com/dp/1087884616/ref=cm_sw_em_r_mt_dp_U_9Zl9EbD778DYV